This book belongs to

____

Bozy Series

Illustrated by Jack Button
Cover Design and Layout by Praise Saflor

ISBN 979-8-218-16089-0 (Hardcover)
979-8-9879108-0-1 (Softcover)

Welcome to the Burnt City

PERSIA

by Mahsan Boogert

Art by Jack Button

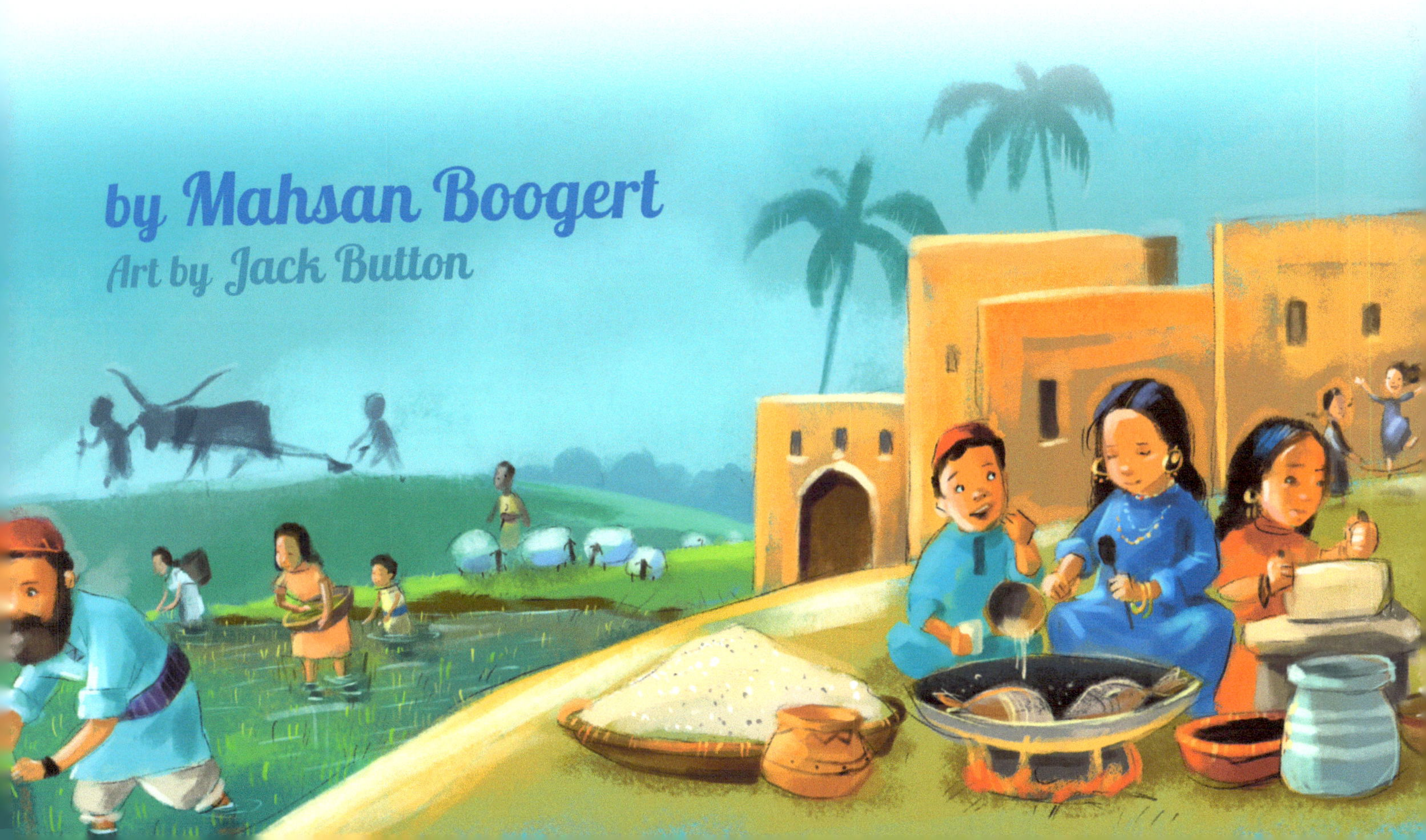

Hello friends!

Do you see the cute goat on this vase?

That's me, Bozy!

Can you believe this vase is 5000 years old?

Do you want to know where it was found?

Then come with me to the Land of Persia, and let me show you the city where the vase was discovered.

Here we are at the entrance to Burnt City.

Do you think this is how Burnt City
looked 5000 years ago?
No way! It was so different!

No one has been seen around here for thousands of years.

Some archeologists think that people left
Burnt City because of weather conditions.

Strong winds and not enough rain made it difficult to
grow yummy fruits and vegetables.

Wow, check out these awesome archeologists!
They're working **super hard!**
They have already found hundreds of very interesting old objects—
small objects, large objects, and every size in between.
Some dishes that were found even had traces of food on them!

I love helping archeologists find amazing treasures!

Do you remember this cool vase
I showed you with a picture of me on it?

You know what's super cool?
This vase has not just one, but five pictures of me!
And when you spin the vase, it looks like
I'm jumping around! Archaeologists say this is the very
first animation ever made, which means I might be the
first cartoon character in history!

Whoa, all this spinning is making me feel dizzy!

It makes me so happy to remember
what life was like 5000 years ago.

Here in Burnt City, life was pretty similar to the way it is in cities today. People lived in beautiful homes of different shapes and sizes.
The city was full of excitement, with people shopping and children playing and going to school.

Families loved spending time together and played a lot of games. One of my favorite games was Backgammon. I liked that game. It was shaped like a snake, and I had to know how to add, subtract and multiply in order to win.

It's hard to believe, but this city
was very advanced at that time!

The plumbing was very similar to what cities have now,
except the people used mud to make the pipes
that carried the water from the river to all the homes.

At that time, many people were really good at making pretty plates, bowls, and cups from mud and clay. They made these dishes to use at home and to sell at the markets.

People from other cities in Persia
often came to buy our dishes because they
were so beautiful and well made!

Moms were excellent at doing business!

Another great discovery by the archaeologists was finding old fishing nets and fishing hooks.

Going to the river with my family to catch fish for dinner was always fun.

Look what I just caught!
I think it's my biggest fish ever!

Rice and beans were very popular foods at that time, and archaeologists found all kinds of seeds around the city.

Here's something else about this city: Archaeologists haven't found any swords or axes that were used for fighting, like in other old cities. The people who lived here were happy and peaceful, and they didn't need those kinds of things.

See this pretty necklace
made of gold and precious jewels?

The people who lived here loved making and wearing jewelry, and so much gold and turquoise has been found in the area.

Many people have come from around the world to help discover new things about Burnt City, but there are still many unanswered questions. For example, archaeologists still don't know for sure what language the people spoke back then in Burnt City. This is a big problem because it makes it impossible to read the writings that were discovered.

Today archaeologists call my city Burnt City because they found ashes all over the city.

BOZY

I hope you have enjoyed learning about Burnt City as much as I enjoyed growing up there.

See you on my next adventure!

Interesting notes to parents

Shahr-i Sokhta, known as the Burnt City, is a fascinating place in southeastern Iran that has been designated as a UNESCO World Heritage site. This ancient city was discovered by archaeologists in the 1970s and is believed to be over 5000 years old.

The people who lived in the Burnt City were part of an advanced urban society that had complex systems of architecture and water management. With a population of around 4000 people, the city was a hub for trade and commerce.

Exciting discoveries have been made by archaeologists at the Burnt City, including a vast collection of pottery and clay figurines. One of the most famous artifacts found there is a vase with a series of drawings that, when spun, creates the illusion of a leaping goat. This is considered to be the oldest example of animation in the world.

However, despite its wealth and technological advancement, Burnt City was abandoned around 3300 BCE. Some archaeologists believe that harsh weather conditions, such as strong winds and lack of rain, made it difficult to grow crops and forced people to leave.

It's interesting to note that in Farsi, "Bozy" means goat. Also, in 1935, the country that is now known as Iran was officially changed from its previous name, Persia.

The original picture of the vase found in Burnt City.

Image by Emesik, via Wikimedia Commons

About the Author

Mahsan is a medical doctor, working in neuroscience research for most of her career. She is a Persian/American and has lived in the U.S. for 23 years. Following her passion for life and historical places, she has begun writing educational books for children. Mahsan's purpose in writing is to pique children's interest in learning about historical places. This inspiring travel-based series focuses on UNESCO sites and monuments all over the world. Mahsan's goal is for her books to inspire young children, offer interesting information about wonderful places, and show how people lived in the past.

More than a hundreds of her Bozy books have already been donated to children's hospitals.

The original picture of the Burnt City.

Image by Unesco.org

www.ingramcontent.com/pod-product-compliance
Ingram Content Group UK Ltd.
Pitfield, Milton Keynes, MK11 3LW, UK
UKHW060112300726
14090UKWH00002B/146
9798987910801